BOA
EDITIONS LTD

THE HEAVEN-SENT LEAF

THE HEAVEN-SENT LEAF

Poems by
KATY LEDERER

AMERICAN POETS CONTINUUM SERIES, NO. 114

BOA EDITIONS, LTD. ❧ ROCHESTER, NY ❧ 2008

First Edition
08 09 10 11   7 6 5 4 3 2 1

For information about permission to reuse any material from this book please contact
The Permissions Company at www.permissionscompany.com or e-mail permdude@
eclipse.net.

Publications by BOA Editions, Ltd.—a not-for-profit corporation under section 501 (c) (3)
of the United States Internal Revenue Code—are made possible with funds from a variety
of sources, including public funds from the New York State Council for the Arts, a state
agency; the Literature Program of the National Endowment for the Arts; the County of
Monroe, NY; the Lannan Foundation for support of the Lannan Translations Selection
Series; the Sonia Raiziss Giop Charitable Foundation; the Mary S. Mulligan Charitable
Trust; the Rochester Area Community Foundation; the Arts & Cultural Council for Greater
Rochester; the Steeple-Jack Fund; the Ames-Amzalak Memorial Trust in memory of Henry
Ames, Semon Amzalak and Dan Amzalak; the TCA Foundation; and contributions from
many individuals nationwide.

See Colophon on page 64 for special individual acknowledgments.

Cover Design: Steve Smock
Interior Design and Composition: Richard Foerster
Manufacturing: Thomson-Shore
BOA Logo: Mirko

Library of Congress Cataloging-in-Publication Data

Lederer, Katy.
  The heaven-sent leaf / Katy Lederer. — 1st ed.
     p. cm. — (American poets continuum series ; no. 114)
  ISBN 978–1–934414–15–6 (pbk.)
  I. Title.

PS3612.E3417H43 2008
811'.6—dc22
                                    2008019128

BOA Editions, Ltd.
Nora A. Jones, Executive Director/Publisher
Thom Ward, Editor/Production
Peter Conners, Editor/Marketing
Glenn William, BOA Board Chair
A. Poulin, Jr., Founder (1938–1996)
250 North Goodman Street, Suite 306
Rochester, NY 14607
www.boaeditions.org

NATIONAL
ENDOWMENT
FOR THE ARTS

State of the Arts

NYSCA

Contents

The Heaven-Sent Leaf

I listen to money singing. It's like looking down
From long French windows at a provincial town,
The slums, the canal, the churches ornate and mad
In the evening sun. It is intensely sad.

—Philip Larkin, "Money"

The Heaven-Sent Leaf

The speculation of contemporary life.
The teeming green of utterance.

To feel this clean,
This dream-éclat.

There is, in the heart, the hard-rendering profit.
As if we were plucking the leaves from the trees.

Let us think of the soft verdure of the spirit of this age as now inside
of us and swollen by spring rain.
To imagine oneself as a river.

To imagine oneself as a stretch of cool water,
Pouring into a basin or brain.

And if one knows one is not free?
One crawls from the back of the head to the river

And places one's pinkie oh so cautiously in.

Me, a Brainworker

Me, a brainworker toiling in pristine white hallways.
Abnormal, aboriginal, endemic to this site.
Some people sell their wares outside.
In the pulsating light of Times Square they are singing.
In their noses and nipples, the glinting of rings.
Let us call them unoriginal.
Let us call them all these awful things.
The busy unoriginals are throwing out their trash,
But on this lovely parchment they are writing priceless poems.
They suppose that by such rendering they'll be remembered after
    death.
They suppose that by such influence their souls will sing eternally.
In the hallways, we are killing time,
Its blood now thick and lurid on the freshly painted walls.

In the Flower Store Next Door

The object in the poem you must focus on is me.
Here in the poem I am, and in the flower store next door
Are wilting daisies, cups of breakfast blend,
And dark, expensive chocolates you may purchase if you please.
We are watching in the flower store our weight, and so we do not
    eat,
But wrap the wilting daisies up in happy flowering trees.
In the branches of these trees, the self will grow and grow till
    plucked.
Once plucked, the happy self will run, the parts will move in unison,
    at once!
Ta-wee, ta-wee, the happy self!
And if one knows one is not free?
I love you, reader, may I say?
I've brought you all these presents, which I've placed beneath this
    flowering tree:
Bright red box, bright blue box, and a small vial of Botox.

The Tender Wish to Buy This World

The tender wish to buy this world.
The shedding of leaves from the wallet of morning.
Down low by the bridge in this city of money,
I will take up this axe, shatter gently this greed.
We are thinking of our heartfelt need,
Our man, his brain dreaming atop the clean pillow.
In the wallet of his soul he files the crisp new bills of morning.
This old depression, when the world will stretch, a field of deep
  ravines.
O Pale Pill, O Obsequious Friend to the needy and nixed, to the
  novitiates who play this mise en scène . . .
O Smotherer.
O Ploughshare.
O Savior and Deranger
Of the Senses.

A Nietzschean Revival

I thought that I was almost lost.
Or overwrought.
Or rotten.
As I stroked with thin quivering fingers this harp,
The tongue-perturbed minions came running amok,
Their scaffolded ears waiting isolately for the word that would deign
    to leave heaven.
In the morning, when I manufacture lyrics on these listless keys,
When the money and its happy apparatus do call and lure,
Do call and lure . . .
These poets speak of capital as if they had the least idea.
I ask you: what do poets know of capital?
Across this harp, their fingers play a Nietzschean revival.
I envy them their will to power.

The Genius of Time

How much time do we waste in this way?
With this wish to be penniless, free?
I am feeling these, the confines of the spirit, so I must give in.
To this scene: of a boy in a sandbox, now playing,
His castle is drying to wind.
He thinks that time belongs to him,
That time does not annihilate according to its ancient will.
He stands in the box, his palms out, the loud wind passing over his
      fingers.
Within his small fingers, the granules of pleasure.
Within his small pleasure, the granules of need.
Let us slake this mind to nothingness,
This body, then, to nothingness.
Let us call this the genius of time.

A Sad Harp

My little instrument, my denouement,
Pass me through to this fine place of whimsy.
I am dreaming in my head of heart, my heart then of my head.
I am dreaming in my head of books,
Of books now bent, their words destroyed.
Are we thinking of this form as harm, we derelict, we deadly?
In the basement the doctor is just getting in.
I am going downstairs to receive my first treatment.
Replacement of the brain by heart, the heart, then, by the brain.
What medical audacity.
This doctor man, this doctor man.
His hands are now playing this sad little harp.
His hands are now playing this harp.

A Congeries of Feeling

A congeries of feeling, a derogatory scene.
Here in the pumped up brain, here in
The brain pumped up with longing.
Along the bright periphery of all that is the world, this fame.
Fama: a creature of many tongues drooling.
Her spittle: the colors now streaking the sky.
Let us think now of the moon as gone,
The sun rising up to the rafters.
We are sleeping here, young as we are and so lovely.
We are sleeping here, dead as the nails in the doors.
We are crafted as we are, we are a congeries of feeling.
This *Fama* will breathe on our fluttering eyes
Before she departs in her white wedding train.

A Flush Forest

If the price is right, let's have a go.
At life or at love or at who all what knows.
In the dream, I am falling.
In the dream, I am calling.
Yoo hoo. Yoo hoo.
What language we learn and forever we run?
What hill in the dream, then, eternally climb?
Up and up I am moving, but never arrive.
What then is the goal?
What then shall we make of the newly born foal,
Who is straining his way up to heaven?
When the forest is green, we come into our wealth.
When the forest is green and the wealthy leaves grow.

In the Hole

I am walking through the money trees, and here a little bough,
Or bow.
I handle it and straddle it, and take a little bow—
Just
To love yourself, honey, put your claw on the table.
Just
To love oneself, honey, kinda lopsided, loamy.
I am standing on the corner, here, the corner of my life.
My thumb is out. The sun is out.
The verbiage like foliage is increasing as the weather wanes.
The sum of the parts equals less than the whole.
Or the howl. Or the how.
Or the hole.

Brainworker

To learn to keep distance.
To learn to keep drear managerial impulse away from the animal
    mind.
Along the dark edge of this reason. Along the dark edge of this
    mind's little prison, inside of its bars now a silky white cat.
Howling.
Crawling in its little cage.
Inside of its cage is the bright light of morning.
Inside of its cage is the light of disease.
To learn to be an animal. To learn to be that primal.
To know who will slip you the fresh dish of milk.
To long for your manager's written approval.
So soon am I up for my year-end review?
The moon above settles into its shadow.
I am howling at you.

Financial Release

To avoid the whole mendacious thing.
To sign yet another financial release.
Your arms collapse against my knees.
My knees are two pigeons, checked wings now aflutter,
Orange-red eyes like small, derogatory suns.
We are standing here dually.
Not wanting to do.
Not wanting to draw our tired bodies up stairs,
To the freshly cleaned desk and the long, covered window,
Its curtains so perfectly evenly drawn.
To look out at the sky: an insurrection of good worker's eyes.
To place one's eyes upon the clouds . . .
Enthroned upon ephemera.

Black, the Surface of the Mind

Black, the surface of the mind.
But true.
I want to call my poem "Black,
The Surface of the Mind."
I want to steal away at night,
I want to call my poem "White,
The Surface of the Mind."
To look out at the landscape drenched in rain and see the surest
    thing:
Laughing girl with a black prophylactic umbrella, her eyes newly
    minted by night.
Worker Night:
Please mint this mind to white.
The surface of the mind is black.
I want to call my poem "White, the Surface of the Mind."

The Business

Let us stop this fraught analysis and get on with the business.
To walk through pristine hallways and observe the little fingers go.
They click and clack, they click and clack.
The sad smiling faces, like clowns'.
The reason that a person would sit down as if to pray
And then just type the mystic day away—
These white walls,
These blue windows.
In some weather, gray.
What this freedom, this river, this emerald-green flow?
Why are we laughing now,
We can't let go?
Why are we laughing now?

The Dead-Level

Beneath this damp light, now receiving a facial.
The emulsifying powers of the white, the blue, the money green.
A peacock feather steaming me.
Beneath this eye, Lord, let us pray.
For beauty, for regality.
The poets standing, one by one.
I lie here, shaking, all alone, the cosmetician in the hall.
Lord, let it cover me, this sheet.
Immaculate particulate.
I hide here in your cleanliness.
The poets standing, one by one.
What shall I make of them, beneath this light?
Their hair is white, their eyes are white, their skin is porcelain white.

The Concubine

There is something unknitting, some weak bit of skin.
Here at the back of the head, here this whim.
Within all these words, if the words are a thicket, we are willing, the
     blessed ones say, to hack through.
Within the brain coiling, the concubine's limbs.
She stretches and yawns.
See, her hands are white spiders!
Grasping.
Wanting what they cannot have:
Release,
A sudden opening
The light outside forgiving.
Forgive this woman of her sins.
Her coinage: *concubinage.*

Morning Song

You color all. Is this longing?
Or private.
Is it private to speak in the morning,
The birdsong like knives?
We sit on this bench while this wind swirls and billows.
This setting is love, yet we sit on this bench, yet we listen to
        birdsong.
This color, your brain, which is bluer than water.
I touch it, your brain, which is cooler than water.
I wonder, your brain, when it falters, will it be so cold?
We buffet one another with our bodies, with our slackened
Hearts. I put myself in it, your body, which aches.
I put myself in it, your brain,
Which is cooler than water.

A Heavenly Body

The earth is a dollar and the moon is a silvery coin
Denomination indeterminate, its imprint rubbed to nearly gone.
Let us free, love, this heavenly body,
As crafted and dumb as all minted desire.
Does the moon receive her meteors with gall or dull sanguinity?
Is she angry? Is she edified?
Does the moon crawl into bed at night, as drunk and relentless as
    any kept woman,
The covers like nothing on top of her legs?
Between these high mountains runs a pass blasted through by the
    movements of water and indebted plateaus.
Imagine it widening, eternally, as the owl will fly or flower bloom.
And so I am imagining the darkness of the avenues,
Long silences between us.
Imagine, Love, the patience of the moon.

Broken Bank

You were thinking about something as luscious and royal as a
    dumbbell,
Small and cold, about to tilt, then smash to silver coins.
You were thinking about something so illogical and blissful,
You grew fraught as a fine temporality.
What did I say?
That to have is not yet to have taken possession.
What's the world that it has come to this?
Greenish-gray, colored safely, and impossible to counterfeit?
We governors or actors.
Dear & Dear.
What is it, really, that we fear?
Of the loss that we accrued,
I think that silver cuffs will do.

Three Poems

Because of Passion or Coincidence

Because of passion or coincidence, they must be they.
Because of passion or coincidence, the stricken lovers wept and said
     adieu to you and let us do what we have to do, which is to be
     gone.
Because of passion or because of coincidence, the tides were thrift
     coming, the sun was thrift shining,
And everything died.

Believe Me

Believe me, you are lucky.
You have been nothing—.
In intervals you become a man.
You are, for days and for years, unbearable.

The Day Has Been Over for My Sake

The day has been over for my sake.
These hours fall under the meek yellow shadow of Saturn.
I fell under the sway of the slowest and seventh of planets,
What some say must then be the distant and dull one,
And how I agree.

Morning Song

It is simply a matter of syntax:
"I." "Love." "You."
It is simply a matter of order.
The simplest words work the best for the complex emotions:
"Love." "Gone." "Loss."
It is morning and we lie here on this clean, white, pleated double
  bed.
We are waiting for the sunrise to unmask us of our sleep.
It is lyrical to dream like this.
We ones who climb like primates up through sleep at night to dream
  of light.
I dream of you. Black Suitor, gone, like sleep.
Like vapid, nothing dreams.
At night these objects take on cast of shadow, yet we sleep.
At night we feel this nothing-new, this tongue-loll, this exigent
  sinew, and I think we must deceive ourselves.

Parable of Times Square

We meet in this country, beneath the damp light at the world-
    famous fair,
Where life is meaningful and dreadful.
The conglomerates show off their wares,
Which will help us when we're sick of work and heading for the
    train.
I hate to be alone. The solitude of Brooklyn.
But outside, now framed by the window, a couple.
They stare at one another over pork chops and beer.
I call you on the telephone. I call to hear
Your muffled voice. "People aren't the be-all and end-all of one
    another's lives," you say.
Between these tender hemispheres, in the space of our gender, the
    divine reaches down like a hook.
Must it be such a hardship, then, to hoist ourselves up to the
    conscious interior?
Are we so cleanly spoken, here, that all has been said by two bodies,
    alone in the dark,
Their brains electrified, their tongues in one another's mouths?

Intimacy

These three bridges, like the brain, lit up and heading out toward
    Brooklyn.
I am slumped in the cab, thinking heady thoughts of heady things.
Like an ostrich. Or like an intellectual thriller.
For example, *Den of Thieves*, in which the arbitrageur Michael
    Milken is at first defined by a healthy ambition that later in the
    story turns to plot-driving greed.
It's as if his most natural desire to do good had over many years
    metastasized, crackling over the phone lines, hiding out in the
    backseat of his de rigueur black limousine, via messenger across
    the Park, his pulmonary conscience pumping darkly in his
    greedy heart . . .
Like a toddler hiding grimly in a closet or a hamper.
Or like the king who fled the palace on the hill that's now ablaze.
Which explains, I guess, the fighter jets that circle overhead,
The surfeit of broadband, as well as this beautiful bed now bereft of
    our lowly ambition.
I'm lying here, there's no one else, and the flowers that you've given
    me are wilting in the Slurpee cup.
There is ambient noise.
Noise of jet planes,
Desire.

The Flower of Life

1.

To keep an assignation with oneself, one must, as a matter of course,
    break in two.
There is you in the snow by the banks of the river, your lips cold and
    blue,
Your hands fulminating with your first true love.
And then me, in the bed, under cotton white covers,
Reading a novel of manners and tragic romance,
Written in a classic style,
Each sentence wrought with great clarity and deliberation,
And yet with a sincerest rage
At the man, who is deeply in love with a woman
He feels it would be condemnably improper to have.
And so he hangs back, marries swiftly and wrongly a betrothed he
    does not love,
Spends his years on the sloped banks of the river of his life,
Observing the current as it eddies and swells with his passionate loss . . .

2.

Today, from the bridge, the East River is sparkling.
The money is swirling around the tall buildings like tides or like
  tithes,
And I wonder, does anyone swim in this river, I wonder, does anyone
  pray?
The legs are mimetic of the mind's locomotion.
You have told me to meet you at Broadway and 6th, and because it's
  a beautiful day
I've decided to walk the several miles from Cadman Plaza to our
  meeting place.
This bridge, I think, is like a church,
With two vaulted arches per buttress beneath which
The cars and pedestrians travel.
In the middle of the summer, one will often ache to get away,
To swim in a river, to pray in a church,
To place one's hands around one's face, propel oneself
Toward some ecstatic union.

Suffer

The Self, just fuck the Self and watch it bleed.
(And not a tourniquet.)

The memory, like glass, across the faded light of atmosphere, of what
    it was to breathe in immaculate air.
And you, gesturing.

You
With your come hither look and your chattering mouth, a voracious
    machine.

The beauty in this wretched place is wheat and oil and interest rate.
It is constant, so what do you care?

Nothing of me, of my
Self.

Nothing of your
Selves.

The Trees are alive and they hate us.

The Intellect Can Only Talk About Wisdom

You have never shed leaves, but you leave.
You are treelike, a long-deranged stump, you grow giant.
Your arms splayed,
Your arrow-sharp head in the God-hole.
In your thick trunk a pump.
Your tongue spitless, your millions of follicle eyes
Glaring barren and useless.
You are spiteful in sunlight,
While at night, in the profligate face of the moon, you bask cold and
    majestic,
Your silhouette cracking the sky.
I wonder if you know of pain.
O Svelte One, without you, what this terrible sun
Beaming plentiful over the world?

The Rose, the Ring

This is a parable of marriage, see?
The rose, the ring, the tolling bell.
The toiling belle.
The man in need of hunting and the gold in need of digging:
Why, we are the regular Captains of Industry!
What we're thinking, we're thinking:
The world is a cage.
What we're thinking, we're thinking:
The world is a money safari.
At night the thoughts fall one by one
Like diamonds to the floor.
We sweep them up, the little jewels,
The little bastard trinkets.

Brainworker

What's the narrative gist?
I am thinking in pairs.
Of a girl, *of a girl.* Philosophically pure.
In her eyes, an empty willingness.
This dollar, put it in her hands, *her hands.*
This quarter, put it in her eyes, *her eyes.*
Her eyes now rolling quarterly.
Along the wall, this carpet, tucked.
Along the sill, this trillium.
An echo, she sits upright, straight.
As if to play the lettered keys.
But these are typist's hands, her hands.
To play her heart, to play her brain, to play her silvery eyes.

Against the Gate

Before the bell tolls,
She must run.

Through garden plot and broken gate.

Against the gate,
The devil has come.

The push of his fingers on the cast-iron rung.

The entrance, the last to have entered
Defendants

Commence with sudden diligence to dream.

The iron in its fire is hot,
The cello in its coffin, quit

And all around the rooftops
Sighs of jaundiced women.

The Apperceptive Mass

Systemic and assembled with great calm.
On the face of one
Who goes into the silent place—
Who goes into the silent place,
Before the inner temple,
And aspires.
Who goes,
That presence, in the den,
An even-tempered lens through which
The transmittal of all that is beautiful goes.
We are hushed in our external sense
Our inner hearts are
Rockets.

The Eternal One

Can he live another way?
With this mystery, this nothing, love.
The royal song of triumph over longing.
The clouds cover him as a cherub in ivory fire.
The rowdy—what?
Eternal One, I have nothing but a bed and a bill in my hand
For the money has made a great gash
In the gnarled, forked river,
Washed down by the mental relation between us—
Eternal One, shoot beyond me, and he can live another way
Constituted as wind or rain
In a mystical basin or tomb
Laced with basest emotion.

The Rapture

I was hunting the thing in order to deface it.
I had set myself up for the rapture,
Was waiting to retire on a soft pelt, a dowager—
High up on the mountain, low down on the hill.
On the financial side, I was run through with leather.
I had submitted my bill.
They said of me, "she is soft and cold."
This was a form of transgression.
I was waiting for my recompense.
Their system doused me.
Their system let my anger bleed
Like a bee-sting or weathervane pointing belatedly
Out toward the last wind's direction.

In the Seafold, Savings, I Have None

I prefer to see them during life—
If life could be better than a shellfish shucked
By your father or some other one.
Your father was the one who left me
Dry and shelved,
Convalescent and needlessly bludgeoned.
Oh conceited or whatever,
Oh eclectic as I find myself
No more than some fucked dowager.
I can slough off my arm, look,
I can slough off, like rain, ingenuity, the genuine.
In developing parameter, in the seafold, savings,
I have none.

The General Drift

I am taken by the minister
He lays his soul to rest.
He is clean as a dove and is lovely.
Like the general drift,
He is caught, as if in a net.
Welted with his longing
For his archangelic mother,
Like a people or father
He loses her among the waves.
In his oceanic, misspent youth
He saw her as a slave,
But then retained her
As his concubine.

Brainworker

The material needs of the fish, their lobotomized wishes—
Where brains once were, their senses are to be.
This aquarium confinement,
Hear the awful racket of their want.
To spy them in the afternoon,
To loosen up the noggin.
And when the day is finally done, the fish now floating, fast asleep—
You come for me, my brother, my forsaken one, dear Nighttime:
The world is where we go to work.
Love, let us hide ourselves.
The carapace, the steaming crepes.
The fish now singing in their sleep,
And all around them water, and this rim.

The Uxorious Bounty

1.

Resist. Resist:
Dehind, dehist.
Return the clear glass to the kitchen forthwith.
Engage what you see in your soul, as in marriage.
Discover the world as an oven, your mother a witch.
Your mother will roast you.
Your mother will eat you, sweet crisp skin and bones!
She knows how delectable little girls are.
You'll be baked like a pastry then broiled like a ham.
Your mother is waiting.
Her body is famished.
Dearest child:
Let us trim you to beauty.

2.

Children, children everywhere,
And not a drop to drink.
I cannot think.
My brain is stopped up with *the children, the children.*
Let us clean them, their eyeballs, their sad little mouths.
Let us clean them with our nether parts, we women.
The men were once children,
We had to admit them.
They'd cry and spit up
Before killing the world.
The drain is now opened—
Dearest child:
Break this water, then run.

Schadenfreude

The vacant sameness of this schadenfreude,
Shameful world for rent.

So show the world your typist's hands
And see what kind of Ugly.

Now waiting for the King to come,
His Majesty in robes. . . .

Now waiting for the Prince to come, the Princess: you,
The Queen blown up.

Now think yourself to smithereens.

What structure lies beneath these words,
A cottage or a kingdom?

Between these words, long vacancy.
And yet this house is not for rent.

An Animal

Black, derogatory.
How. How. How.
And why.
A feeling. Pen it in.
To form it, to make it a subject, a nugget,
To pen the monstrosity in.
To take a metaphor from daily life of what none of us knows.
To make a shape of it, imagine it,
To make of it
A thing.
To want very badly to pen the thing in,
Make it stay,
Like an animal, howling.

Parable of House and Broom

The gap between wanting and having is
Great.

What does the house care when brooms
Shake?

The minaret
When the sky breaks

Over it?

Nothing.

The tall trees are whispering to the wind
That they are comely.

The wind brings its tidy joy
And in its wake,

Removes.

Kept

I dream of being ravished and astonished.

In the big branch,
On the burnished bench—

In the way that arachnids or caricatured figures
Must fuck one another.

Astonish me.

In the pitch trapezoidal room,
Before dark falls,
The catastrophe, waiting.

Kept by it, caged up,
The soul is then girlish.

The moon that is yellow
Reneges us.

This Long Wait for the Brain to Unravel Its Bankroll

This long wait for the brain to unravel its bankroll.
We are going to meet our friends: Greedy and Ugly.
Now just give me this thing. Let me into this club.
Lay the balls of your feet on the desk.
In this clean pied-à-terre, this fear.
The birds outside asinging.
What feelings thus we adumbrate?
What language, thus? What kind of hate?
Is hatred an emotion, yes?
What is it that sings in this gentrified brain?
What favor, what river, what emerald-green flow?
Why are we laughing now? We can't let go?
Why are we laughing now?

So Some of Us Are Waiting Here

Across the way, across the wood, across the winding bay.
Before, there was a travesty, and now there is a day.
So some of us are waiting here, so some of us, away.
So some of us are waiting here, so some of us, away.
To look out at the landscape drenched in rain and see the surest
    thing.
To move across the landscape drenched in ice,
This glacial settling.
What does this mist, this lost caress—
I know not what to sing.
What does it mean to sing?
This loveliness,
Across the wood,
Across the winding bay.

That Everything's Inevitable

That everything's inevitable.
That fate is whatever has already happened.
The brain, which is as elemental, as sane, as the rest of the
      processing universe is.
In this world, I am the surest thing.
Scrunched-up arms, folded legs, lovely destitute eyes.
Please insert your spare coins.
I am filling them up.
Please insert your spare vision, your vigor, your vim.
But yet, I am a vatic one.
As vatic as the Vatican.
In the temper and the tantrum, in the well-kept arboretum
I am waiting, like an animal,
For poetry.

A Triumvirate

Dilapidation of the spirit as the heart gives in, the mind gives in.
These three, a triumvirate, laughing.
This bitterness breaks me.
This light at the back of the head cracks the notion's façade and
    behind it the mind plays its bric-a-brac music.
To find the right image.
To place one's lips gently atop the flute's metal, to feel it there, cold
    on the mouth.
I have been on this journey for months.
From the back of the head to the river, it hurts.
It hurts.
I am singing.
Oh yes, I am singing.
My mind is at ease.
I will die like this, penniless.

The Unseduced

Like a kettle, a lever, a lathe,
I have used you.
To walk the long avenues,
Rings in the windows,
The casements like coffins
Or coins.
The dusk, an asylum,
The wind
In the spasming leaves—
We must count up
The dowry, Love,
The uxorious bounty
At the crux of our parting.

Acknowledgments

Thanks to the editors of these publications for supporting my work:

The American Poetry Review: "Intimacy," "Parable of Times Square";

The Boston Review: "Morning Song" ('You color all'), "Morning Song" ('It is simply a matter of syntax'), "That Everything's Inevitable," "A Triumvirate";

caffeinedestiny.com: "A Flush Forest," "Brainworker" ('To learn to keep distance'), "The Business," "Brainworker" ('What's the narrative gist'), "So Some of Us Are Waiting Here";

Coconut.com: "The Business," "The Unseduced," "An Animal";

Crowd: "A Nietzschean Revival," "The Apperceptive Mass," "The Eternal One";

CutBank: "The Heaven-Sent Leaf," "In the Flower Store Next Door," "Financial Release";

East Village Poetry Web: "The Rapture," "In the Seafold, Savings, I Have None";

The Harvard Review: "The Tender Wish to Buy This World," "A Sad Harp";

Identitytheory.com: "The Intellect Can Only Talk About Wisdom";

Jacket: "In the Hole";

The Paris Review: "Broken Bank," "The Flower of Life," "The Uxorious Bounty";

Perihelion.com: "Against the Gate";

Tool: "Parable of House and Broom";

Typomag.com: "The General Drift."

Thanks also to Gillian Conoley for soliciting several of these poems for the *Boston Review*'s "Poets Sampler" section, Douglas Messerli for including "The Apperceptive Mass" in *The Gertrude Stein Awards for Innovative American Poetry 2006* (Green Integer, 2008), Rachel Zucker and Arielle Greenberg for including "Three Poems" and "Morning

Song" ('You color all') in their anthology *Women Poets on Mentorship: Efforts and Affections* (University of Iowa Press, 2008), and Joshua Beckman and Matthew Zapruder for including "Suffer" in *State of the Union* (Wave Books, 2008).

Reading undertaken during a 2004 residency at Yaddo inspired me to undertake this sequence; the support of a 2005 Fellowship Award from The New York Foundation for the Arts, a 2005 residency at Yaddo, and a 2007 residency at the MacDowell Colony encouraged me to complete it. Rick Barot, Deedy Lederer, Richard Lederer, Alissa Quart, Mike Scharf, and Monica Youn read different versions of the manuscript. I am grateful for their thought and care. I am also grateful to Thom Ward, Peter Conners, and everyone at BOA for making the entire editorial process a real pleasure.

The term *brainworker*, which denotes a highly educated white-collar worker, is taken from *The Affluent Society*, by John Kenneth Galbraith. The title "The Flower of Life" is taken from *The Age of Innocence*, by Edith Wharton. The title "The Intellect Can Only Talk About Wisdom" is taken from "*Sum*, I Am," by D. W. Winnicott. The line "that fate is whatever has already happened" in "That Everything's Inevitable" is semi-cadged from Lyn Hejinian.

This book's title is taken from the second part of Goethe's *Faust*, in which Mephistopheles has discovered a way to make gold—what alchemists had been seeking to discover for centuries—by printing paper money ("the heaven-sent leaf"). Once Mephistopheles has printed this imaginative money, thereby releasing an impecunious emperor from debt, what we would now term an economic "bubble" ensues; viands, wine, and labor are purchased with nothing so substantial as delusion and credulity. By the end of the story, the proverbial bubble has burst, and the emperor has fallen into ruin.

About the Author

Katy Lederer is the author of the poetry collection *Winter Sex* and the memoir *Poker Face: A Girlhood Among Gamblers*. Currently a poetry editor of *Fence Magazine*, she edited her own magazine, *Explosive*, from 1996 to 2006. Her honors and awards include fellowships from The Iowa Writers' Workshop, Yaddo, the MacDowell Colony, and the New York Foundation for the Arts. She lives in the borough of Brooklyn and worked for many years for a hedge fund.

BOA Editions, Ltd.
American Poets Continuum Series

Colophon

The Heaven-Sent Leaf, poems by Katy Lederer, is set in Adobe Garamond, a digital font designed in 1989 by Robert Slimbach (1956–) based on the French Renaissance roman types of Claude Garamond (ca. 1480–1561) and the italics of Robert Granjon (1513–1589).

The publication of this book is made possible, in part, by the special support of the following individuals:

Anonymous (2)
Alan & Nancy Cameros
Gene & Joyce Clifford
Gwen & Gary Conners
Peter & Sue Durant
Pete & Bev French
Dane & Judy Gordon
Kip & Debby Hale
Peter & Robin Hursh
Willy & Bob Hursh
X. J. & Dorothy Kennedy
Archie & Pat Kutz
Jason D. Labbe
Jack & Gail Langerak
Rosemary & Lewis Lloyd
Donna M. Marbach
Boo Poulin
Steven O. Russell & Phyllis Rifkin-Russell
John Sabat
Vicki & Richard Schwartz
The Wallack Family
Patricia D. Ward-Baker
Pat & Mike Wilder
Glenn & Helen William